James Basire

The Rudiments of Ancient Architecture, in Two Parts

Containing an historical account of the five orders, with their proportions and examples of each from the antiques

James Basire

The Rudiments of Ancient Architecture, in Two Parts
Containing an historical account of the five orders, with their proportions and examples of each from the antiques

ISBN/EAN: 9783337393342

Printed in Europe, USA, Canada, Australia, Japan

Cover: Foto ©ninafisch / pixelio.de

More available books at **www.hansebooks.com**

THE
RUDIMENTS
OF
ANCIENT ARCHITECTURE,
IN TWO PARTS.

CONTAINING

An Historical Account of the FIVE ORDERS, with their Proportions and Examples of each from the ANTIQUES;

ALSO

VITRUVIUS on the Temples and Intercolumniations, &c. of the Ancients.

Calculated for the Use of those who wish to attain a summary Knowledge of the SCIENCE of ARCHITECTURE.

WITH

A DICTIONARY OF TERMS.

ILLUSTRATED WITH TEN PLATES.

LONDON:
PRINTED FOR I. & J. TAYLOR, AT THE ARCHITECTURAL LIBRARY, HOLBORN.
MDCCLXXXIX.

PREFACE.

CUSTOM has established the necessity of a preface, which may also be considered as a privilege, authors enjoying therein liberty to explain, and plead for their labours. Much pleading I am not qualified for, nor perhaps entitled to; I therefore submit to the candor of those, who, by the purchase and perusal of this work, have some claim to pass judgment upon it: the great difference between a perfect work and a good intent, encourages me to explain.

ARCHITECTURE, as a liberal science, and considered as connected with the study of antiquities, is a subject on which every person of taste and reading, at some time or other, has occasion for information; yet that precision in rules necessary to a professional man, is not the kind of knowledge wanted; but something more general which will not fatigue the mind to understand, or burthen the memory to recollect. Under this impression, I make public what was originally designed for mere amusement.

The guide I followed in selecting and illustrating, was, a recollection of the wants I formerly felt, when desirous of a general knowledge of Architecture. Many treatises there are on the subject; but as I chiefly sought amusement, the sight of large and intricate works damped the ardour of enquiry, and more than once repelled the thirst of knowledge. To understand the productions of scientific writers, required an exertion of attention

PREFACE. iii

attention mere amufement ftartled at; however, at laft activity was roufed by the inconvenience of ignorance, and fortunately meeting with Sir W. CHAMBERS's excellent treatife, the path was confiderably fmoothened, and trod with greater pleafure than at firft I expected: from this and other books I was afterwards induced to examine, the following fheets may be confidered as notes or minutes, of what is neceffary to be known by one, whofe defire, as mine was, is rather general information, than of the minutiæ of the fcience.—In this view, I hope there will be found fufficient to give a tolerably precife idea of the five orders, and their feveral parts; the engravings exhibit their general effect, and are felected from antiques which have ever been refpected for their proportion and elegance: thefe, with the deviations of modern times, and the hiftorical account of each order,

A 2 will,

will, I flatter myfelf, render the acquiring a knowledge of the fubject both eafy and entertaining; yet fufficiently accurate to enable a gentleman to fketch any drawing of Architecture, fancy or neceffity may prompt him to have executed, without erring much from the general rules of defign, and from which a workman will readily reduce the fmaller parts to the exactnefs requifite to be worked from.

The frontifpiece fhews each order drawn to the fame height; that their relative proportion and ftrength may be feen at one view.

That information might not ftop at the beginning of the fcience, I have tranflated from Vitruvius, what his excellent pen has recorded, as the rules of the ancients in building their edifices, or temples, the diftribution of columns, and their diminutions. Thefe will,

PREFACE. v

will, I hope, alfo be found ufeful to travellers who vifit the remains of ancient architectural fplendor and magnificence; as in a pocket volume they will have examples of the five orders, with the laws obferved by the ancients in the great outline of their public ftructures, by what name and character each order of building is diftinguifhed, with rules for adjufting the columns; from which, an edifice, though in ruins, may, with confiderable certainty, be reftored to its original form.

I HAVE alfo added a Dictionary, or explanation of terms ufed by artifts, to exprefs the feveral parts of buildings; this will, I hope, affift, as well travellers, as thofe who read the accounts of profeffional men; it will facilitate underftanding their labours, and, of courfe, render them more pleafant.

I HOPE,

I HOPE, in its general acceptance, the title of *Ancient Architecture* will be allowed to the following sheets, though noticing only the Greek and Roman stiles; omitting to mention those very ancient efforts in the science, traces of which remain in Upper Egypt, and in many parts of India, the æra of whose foundation is so remote, that no certainty can be formed of their age; they evidence much labour and magnificence. Also Gothic Architecture I have avoided mentioning, not because I think slight of, or disapprove that light though firm, and grave though pleasant kind of Architecture, of which this country boasts the best and most complete specimens. The effect of awe and reverence this kind of building always produces in the mind, is one of the strongest proofs which can be given of its propriety and fitness, for large sacred buildings.

These

These I have avoided, confining myself to the Greek and Roman stiles, which may truly be called classical, and which are in most general request and use.

Upon the whole, my endeavour is intended more for the gentleman than the artist.—How far I have succeeded in the several particulars, I leave to others to determine, assuring them I have spared no pains to be both accurate and useful.

The portrait in the title page, is of the celebrated James Stuart, Esq. generally known by the appellation of *Athenian Stuart:* this is copied from an impression of a plate intended for his promised volume. From a personal knowledge of Mr. Stuart, I can say, this is an extraordinary good likeness, which from my respect to the man, as well as to a great artist, I beg leave to multiply.

RUDIMENTS

OF

ANCIENT ARCHITECTURE.

PART the FIRST.

THE study of Architecture has, in every enlightened age, and by every civilized nation, been held in very honourable esteem; as a necessary and pleasing science, and of evident utility.

When we consider it as improved by the Greeks about the time of Pericles, its perfection and beauty, how conspicuously it exhibited the liberality, splendour, and magnificence of those concerned in erecting structures, the remains of which

which aftonifh us; and how highly flattering it was to the mind of man in an age of fplendour, to raife edifices which fhould ftrike beholders with admiration; it excites little furprife that every attention fhould have been given to the ftudy of architecture, and that its profeffors fhould have received the moft liberal encouragement from men of tafte, anxious for renown.

Persons of the moft exalted ftations have honoured it as ftudents, and thought it not beneath them to attend to its rules.

In prefent times, among ourfelves, we have inftances of dignified perfons ftudying the rules of architecture, which, united to true tafte, have produced defigns that would honour the genius of the higheft profeffors.

Animated by fuch examples, it is not furprifing the fcience fhould now be regarded with confiderable attention: the frequent tours to Italy, and other parts celebrated for elegant edifices, though now in ruins, have with the love

of,

of, spread a vast knowledge and justness of taste among our nobility and gentry, whose leisure has afforded opportunity for exploring those remains of ancient grandeur; add to this, the great industry and attention of some of our most celebrated architects in examining and delineating these standards of art. The liberal encouragement these have experienced, has enabled them to publish their labours, which now furnish ourselves at home, with most advantages acquirable from visits to Rome, Athens, &c.

THE important use of this science, and the elegant accomplishment connected with its study, have almost rendered a knowledge of it requisite to the education of men of fashion and taste. My intention is not to enter into a detail of encomiums on the art; but merely to remark its great utility, and by what high characters its study has been, and is honoured.

I PROCEED, therefore, to my more immediate

mediate defign, which is, to give a fhort hiftorical account of the five orders of Architecture of the ancients; which muft be confidered as the bafis of true proportion.

The great antiquity of building is felf-evident: " When men firft felt the inclemencies of the feafons, it had its beginning, and has fpread wherever the feverities of climate demand fhelter or fhade: it is to be traced in the Indian's hut, and the Greenlander's cave; and fhews in thofe barbarous parts of the globe, from what mean original it rofe to its prefent glory." And perhaps the neighbourly affiftance required in erecting the meaneft fence againft the inclemency of the weather, was the firft introduction of civil fociety: thus a number of habitations were formed together, and men, in confequence, had mutual converfation and intimacy. It is eafy to conceive, that, in this early ftate of fociety, genius had expanded but little; the firft efforts were fmall, and the ftructure fimple;

simple; perhaps no more than a number of trees leaning together at the top (in the form of a cone), interwoven with twigs, and plaiftered with mud, to exclude air, and complete the work. In this early period, we may fuppofe each defirous to render his own habitation more convenient than his neighbours, by improving on what had been already done: thus in time, obfervation, affifting that natural fagacity inherent even in uncultivated minds, led them to confider the inconveniences of the round fort of habitation, and feek others more fpacious and convenient in the fquare form.

THIS improvement introduced the neceffity of fupports for the crofs beams, which were to fuftain the roof: the trunks of trees were fo ready an application, we cannot fuppofe they hefitated long in their choice. Thus from the nature of things arofe the idea of what we now call columns, which have from time to time under-

undergone many changes, and at laſt have produced thoſe elegant pillars which we term the orders of architecture.

To attempt producing an authority or origin for every ſpecies of ornament attending the orders, would be wandering in a maze of uncertainty, attended with much labour, and little recompenſe: the general parts may, with more certainty, have their origin pointed out.

The *Plinth*, it is very reaſonable to imagine, was, at firſt, ſimply a ſquare tile or ſtone, placed under the trunk of the tree or primitive column, to prevent rotting, to which it was expoſed from the conſtant moiſture of the earth; it alſo ſerved as a more firm and ſolid footing to the column.

The *Torus*, or ſwell above the plinth, may have originated from the root or lower part of the tree being thicker than the part above, which alſo fixed it more firmly on the plinth; or, as by ſome it is conjectured to have been only a rope or bandage round the trunk, to prevent its splitting.

The *Shaft* of the column has been already noticed.

The idea of the *Capital*, I think, may have originally been suggested by some tree, whose arms spreading just above where it was necessary the upper parts should be cut off (to be of a proper length), the swell of the arms very likely gave the first idea of the swell of the capital, which was also attended with this advantage, by being broader on the top, it was better formed for receiving the works above.

The *Abacus* was certainly no more than a tile or stone, placed with intent to throw off the water, and prevent its sinking into the column, which would have endangered the duration of the building.

The *Astragals* and *Fillets* were bandages to bind the column.

The *Architrave* we may conceive to be

be the beams neceffary to hold or unite the columns together.

The *Frize* was a neceffary addition to give height within.

The *Cornice*, and its ornaments, were the ends or outer edge of the roof and rafters.

The Denteles, Triglyphs, Modillions, &c. moft likely were accidental hints improved, when to ufefulnefs was wifhed to be added ornament.

The orders as now executed, are five, and range as follow: the *Tufcan*, the *Doric*, the *Ionic*, the *Corinthian*, and the *Compofite*; which are diftinguifhed from each other by the column with its bafe and capital, and by the entablature.

The *Tufcan* order is characterized by its plain and robuft appearance, and is therefore ufed only in works, where ftrength and plainnefs are wanted; it has been ufed with great effect and elegance in that durable monument of ancient

cient grandeur, the Trajan column at Rome; indeed, general confent has eftablifhed its proportions for fuch purpofes, beyond all others.

THE *Doric* poffeffes nearly the fame character for ftrength as the Tufcan, but is enlivened by its peculiar ornaments; the triglyph, mutule, and guttæ or drops, under the triglyph; thefe decorations characterize the Doric order, and in part are infeparable from it. Its proportions recommend it where united ftrength and grandeur are wanted.

THE *Ionic* partakes of more delicacy than either of the former, and therefore, as well as on account of its origin, is called Feminine, and not improperly compared to a matronic appearance; it is a medium between the mafculine Tufcan and Doric, and the virginal flendernefs of the Corinthian :—the boldnefs of the capital, with the beauty of the fhaft, makes it eligible for porticos, frontifpieces, entrances to houses, &c. Denteles were first added to the cornice of this order.

THE *Corinthian* possesses more delicacy and ornament than any other order; the beauty and richness of the capital, with the delicacy of the pillar, render it very properly adapted, when magnificent elegance is required: it is frequently used for internal decoration to large or state rooms; the appearance is of virginal delicacy, and gay attire.

THE *Composite* order is the same as the Corinthian in its proportions, and nearly alike in its effects: the addition of the modern Ionic volute to the capital, gives a bolder projection. It is applicable in the same manner as the Corinthian.

THE examples chosen to exhibit the effects, and give a general idea of the proportions of the several parts at one view, are selected from antiques; these compositions having stood the test of ages, for their symmetry and effect: the modern proportions

portions in the descriptive account, I have taken from Sir WILLIAM CHAMBERS's useful Treatise on Civil Architecture. To the examples shewn in the plates, the measurements are figured to each particular member; thus, by comparing them, the variations of the moderns from the ancients may be easily known.

THE measurements are in minutes, that is, one-half of the lower diameter divided into thirty parts or minutes, which method, having fewer calculations than any other, is preferable: the projections are measured from the perpendicular of the superior and inferior parts of the column.

OF THE

FIVE ORDERS.

OF the TUSCAN order little hiftoric can be faid; its plainnefs of ornament gives it the firft place in moft treatifes: there is no regular example of this among the remnants of antiquity. Vitruvius in an indiftinct manner has mentioned the general proportions, but through his whole book does not refer to one ftructure of this order. The Trajan column at Rome is reckoned of the Tufcan order, though it has eight diameters for the height; and the capital is certainly more ornamented than is confiftent with Tufcan plainnefs. It is fomewhat fingular there fhould be no remains of this order; and were it not for what little Vitruvius has written of it, it certainly might have been loft to the moderns. The plainnefs of its appearance,

appearance, no doubt, caufed it to be neglected at Rome; but in no other place has been difcovered any truly ancient example.

OF the Doric we have many remains of very ancient date, which leads me to think the Tufcan is no other than the Doric more fimplified, or deprived of its ornaments to fuit certain purpofes, where ftrength and cheapnefs were wanted; neverthelefs it is applied with propriety and effect, to the entrance of cities, large gateways, and in military architecture, where a maffive ftrength only is required.

I HAVE felected the profile given by Palladio, he having feen fome remains in Italy, which might lead him to more juft ideas of what the ancients practifed in this order. It certainly derived its name from the people of Tufcany, in Italy, they having firft ufed it.

SIR WILLIAM CHAMBERS gives it the following proportions:

" THE height of the column is fourteen modules,

modules, or feven diameters; that of the whole entablature three modules and a half, which being divided into ten equal parts, three are for the height of the architrave; three for the frize; and the remaining four for the cornice: the capital is in height one module: the bafe, including the lower cincture (which is peculiar to the meafurement of this order) of the fhaft, is alfo one module; and the fhaft, with its upper cincture and aftragal, is twelve modules: in interior decorations, the height of the column may be fourteen modules and a half, or even fifteen modules; which increafe may be in the column only."

Of the Doric order there are many examples ftill remaining; fome of very high antiquity, and of proportions fo diffimilar to the practice of later times, that one cannot help concluding, they were produced before experience had formed the rules of art. In feveral buildings exhibited to us in the ruins of *Pæftum*,

Ionia,

Ionia, and even of *Athens,* the height of the columns does not exceed four diameters, or at moſt four and a half: the low appearance of theſe in large buildings, muſt ſurely convince us uſefulneſs was regarded more than the laws of deſign. Indeed the various examples of the Doric order of theſe uncouth and inelegant proportions, nearly prove this to be the order of columns firſt uſed.

Though the Tuſcan pillar is more plain in the ornaments, and as now practiſed of fewer diameters; yet, as we have neither example, or authority, on which to ſuppoſe it ever much varied from the rules at preſent acknowledged, I think we may conclude it is no other than the Doric order, by being executed plainer (as before obſerved), adapted to more menial ſervices by the inhabitants of Tuſcany.

The Doric order, which is no ſmall mark of its antiquity, has experienced many great changes in its proportions and parts, at one time very low, as before remarked;

marked; afterwards it was allowed six diameters, and in succeeding times eight.

Vitruvius allows this to be the most ancient order, and gives the following account of its origin: " Dorus, the son of Helenis, and the nymph Optyce, built a temple in the ancient city of Argos, to the goddess Juno, which happened to be of this order, but which then had no regular proportions; it derived its name from the patron of the building. This example, or order, was followed by all the cities of Achaia."

" Ion, the son of Xuthus, afterwards built a temple in Asia, to Apollo Paninonius, of this order ; and, to render it more agreeable to the eye, he gave six diameters to the column, being guided therein by the example of nature, which has given to the height of man six times the length of his foot."

Modern practice allows eight diameters, and a base, which was never given to the Doric order by the ancients: this

is

is another mark of its antiquity; for certainly the base is no less proper than elegant.

CONCERNING the flutings, whether they were at first practised or not, is impossible to determine: the remains of this order of the oldest date are fluted. I am inclined to think, when any thing like ornament was wished to be added, the fluting of columns early presented itself. The original columns having been trees, it was the natural effect of a hot climate on their bark to make it crack or divide, which I think would readily give the hint of flutings.

THE Triglyph, a characteristic mark of this order, has more the appearance of art; yet I think, the ends of projecting rafters might produce this effect, or near enough, to be improved into what we at present see them; the places assigned them also corroborate this idea. The ornaments on the metope, or the space between the triglyphs, may have been originally trophies of the Deity, or implements of sacrifice placed there: the bull's skull is peculiar to the Doric order.

The profile here given is from the theatre of Marcellus, which has ever been considered as of just proportion for this masculine order: the measurements are according to MONSIEUR DESGODETZ. The denteles in the cornice belong not so properly to this order as to the Ionic: I have taken the liberty to alter the slope of the corona, which in the original is declining, as it is not generally so practised, having a very heavy effect. It was certainly executed there, on account of some optical reason unknown to us. The column has eight diameters, which is now the general practice: is without a base, but the attic base, or its peculiar one may be used. This example is not fluted; but the base to this order (Plate VII.) shews the manner of a Doric fluted column, which differs from every other, being very shallow, and without any space or fillet between the flutings, which are generally twenty, sometimes twenty-four. There are

are examples among the antiques of the column being fquared off, or wrought with pans, as they are called, inftead of hollows. Of this kind is the temple of Minerva at Syracufe, of very ancient Doric: the pillars are cut in pans or angles, and are without bafes. The temple of Diana at the fame place is alfo in the fame ftyle of Doric.

The modern proportions from the before cited author, are as follow:

" The height of the column, including its capital and bafe, is fixteen modules: the height of the entablature, four modules; which being divided into eight parts, two are for the architrave, three for the frize, and three for the cornice: the bafe is one module in height; the capital thirty-two minutes or a little more."

The Ionic order has the following account of its origin by Vitruvius.

" Ion (the fame as before mentioned) building a temple to Diana, and feeking fome new manner, to render it more elegant,

gant, had recourfe, as before in the Doric order, to the human figure; and gave to this new order a feminine delicacy: thus he was the firft who gave eight diameters to a column, that the afpect might be more pleafing; and that its appearance might be more lofty, he added a bafe, in imitation of a fhoe: the volutes, like locks or plaits of hair, hanging on each fide, he gave to the capital, ornamented with fruits, or flowers in feftoons, and furrows, or flutings down the column were wrought, refembling the folds or plaits of a matron's garment."—"Thus he invented two kinds of columns, in the Doric imitating a manly robuft appearance, without ornament; in the Ionic, regarding a female delicacy, accompanied with ornaments pleafing and elegant."—" Succeeding architects much approving the tafte and ingenuity of this defign, allowed eight diameters and a half to this order."

THIS account of VITRUVIUS points out in what manner another column or order

order of architecture was introduced, an invention which has juftly been celebrated and followed, on account of the beauty and elegance of its parts. Many temples, and other ftructures, have been built of this order in various parts of Greece and Italy.

VITRUVIUS records an anecdote much in praife of the Ionic order, in the following words: " The difficulty attending the proper adjuftment of the mutules, metopes, and triglyphs in Doric ftructures, was fuch, as frequently to be a caufe of much inconvenience and trouble to architects in large buildings, and alfo rendered their afpect confufed and embarraffing; on which account, and the maffy appearance of the Doric column, it was thought improper for facred buildings: of this opinion were Tarchenius and Pytheus, with many ancient architects; alfo the celebrated Hermogenes, who, when he was building the temple of Bacchus at Teos, rejected the Doric, though all the marbles

marbles were ready cut, and in its ſtead
erected a temple of the Ionic order."

From the remains of this very celebrated building the example of this order
here ſhewn is taken: the grandeur of its
appearance will, I flatter myſelf, juſtify
the choice: it is here given as reſtored in
that elegant work the "Ionian Antiquities."

The volute of the capital is now often
executed on an angular plan, the ſame as
in the Compoſite order; ſo that, viewed
every way, it has the ſame appearance:
this differs from the regular antiques; and,
poſſeſſing ſeveral advantages, is ſometimes
to be preferred.

The ſtandard of the modern proportions is as follows:

" The height of the column is eighteen
modules; and that of the entablature four
modules and a half, or one quarter the
height of the column, as in the other orders, which is a trifle leſs than in the regular antique Ionics: the capital is twenty-
one

one minutes; and the bafe thirty minutes in height: the fhaft of the column may be plain, or fluted, with twenty, or twenty-four flutings, whofe plan may be a trifle more than a femicircle, becaufe they then appear more diftinct; and the fillet or interval between them muft not be broader than one third of the breadth of the fluting, nor narrower than one quarter thereof; the ornaments of the capital are to correfpond with the flutings of the fhaft; and there muft be an ove above the middle of each fluting. The entablature being divided into ten equal parts, three are for the architrave; three for the frize; and four for the cornice. In interior decorations, where much delicacy is required, the height of the entablature may be reduced to one fifth of the height of the column.

The CORINTHIAN order, in the opinion of VITRUVIUS, " differs from the Ionic only in its capital; the Ionic capital having no more than one third of the diameter of the column for its height; but the Corinthian capital is allowed one entire diameter, which gives to the column a noble, but delicate grandeur. The other members placed on the Corinthian pillar, are common to the Doric and Ionic orders; for it has no particular fpecies of ornament peculiar to its cornice: fometimes it has the Doric mutules and triglyphs in the architrave; fometimes an Ionic frize, with denteles in the cornice; in a manner, it is no more than a third order, rifen out of the former two, which has nothing peculiar to itfelf, but the capital." The origin of which he thus records:

" A MARRIAGEABLE young lady of Corinth fell ill, and died; after the interment, her nurfe collected together fundry ornaments with which fhe ufed to be pleafed; and putting them into a bafket, placed it near her tomb; and, left they fhould be injured by the weather, fhe covered the bafket with a tile. It happened the bafket was placed on a root of acanthus,
which

which in spring shot forth its leaves; these running up the side of the basket, naturally formed a kind of volute, in the turn given by the tile to the leaves."—" Happily *Callimachus*, a most ingenious sculptor, passing that way, was struck with the beauty, elegance, and novelty of the basket surrounded by the acanthus leaves; and, according to this idea or example, he afterwards made columns for the Corinthians, ordaining the proportions such, as constitute the Corinthian order."

VITRUVIUS, in the foregoing account, forgot the peculiarities of the Corinthian cornice, or, the entablature to that order was not then practised in the manner we find remaining among ancient buildings; for to this cornice, the modillion is ever an attendant.

THE beauty and elegance of this order have rendered it famous, and the many examples existing among the fragments of antiquity, sufficiently evince the great esteem with which it was regarded.

THE

The ravages of cruel and defolating war have not left us one remain of this order, of the many celebrated examples which the city of Corinth poffeffed, where arts of every kind, and particularly architecture, eminently flourifhed and were carried to their perfection. In later times, the conduct of Lucius Mummius, in the deftruction of that polifhed people and city, would have juftly been confidered as the groffeft barbarifm: the temples, the facred buildings were deftroyed, and levelled with the ground; fo that by one ftroke the works of ages were defolated, the labours and ingenuity of thoufands deftroyed, and pofterity deprived of every trace of this order, in the place of its nativity and nurture.— Although Rome would not fuffer Corinth as a rival city, there is little doubt fhe deigned to follow the rules and laws of art eftablifhed by her vanquifhed enemy, efpecially in architecture. The elegance and purity of ftyle in many of her buildings

buildings clearly evince Grecian ingenuity and art.

THE profile here given, is according to PALLADIO's meafurements of the Corinthian pillars to the portico of the Rotunda at Rome: the univerfal celebrity of this ftructure, pointed it out as a proper example.

THE moderns have adapted the following proportions: " The column is twenty modules in height; the entablature five modules; the bafe one module, and may be either Attic or Corinthian: the capital has feventy minutes in height; the proportion of the members of the entablature, is the fame as in the Tufcan and Ionic orders. If the entablature is enriched, the fhaft of the column may be fluted, and the flutings may be filled to one third part of their height with cabling, which will ftrengthen the lower part of the column, and make it lefs liable to injury. In very rich interior decorations, the cabling may be compofed of reeds, ribbands,

ribbands, hufks, flowers, &c. The capital is enriched with olive leaves, as almoft all the antiques at Rome of this order are; the acanthus is feldom employed but in the Compofite order: the entablature to this order may be reduced to two ninths, or one fifth of the height of the column; in which cafe it is beft to ufe the Ionic entablature, or reduce the denteles of the cornice."

The Composite or *Roman* order certainly owes its origin to that conftant folicitude after novelty, which ever renders the mind of man reftlefs in enlightened and highly cultivated ages. The defire of variety and novelty, either of new invention, or combination, certainly engaged the Roman architects to unite with the proportions of the Corinthian order, the ornaments of the Ionic, and by this union to compofe a new order. This order has been handled very feverely by fome critics, whofe palates are pleafed with nothing, which does not relifh
ftrong

ſtrong of the ruſt of high antiquity: theſe have endeavoured to draw on it a ſtigma and diſcredit, it by no means deſerves.—

THE introduction of the modern Ionic volute, and the omiſſion of the upper row of leaves in the capital, certainly give it a more bold and animating aſpect, than that of the Corinthian capital, yet different from any of the other orders, poſſeſſing an elegance and projection very pleaſing, and may be uſed with very agreeable and happy effects.—There are many examples remaining at Rome, which ſhew the general eſtimation of this order there, in the height of its ſplendour and proſperity. In their triumphal arches, it was uſed with good effect, where it produced an agreeable boldneſs, joined to elegance and ornament.

THE example here given is, as it is executed in the triumphal arch, erected to the honour of Veſpaſian and Titus at Rome; the juſtneſs of the proportions, with

with the elegance of the ornaments, mark it as a proper ftandard for the Compofite order.

The proportions of the moderns are as follow: " The height of the column is twenty modules; and that of the entablature five modules; the capital has feventy minutes in height; the bafe meafures the fame as in the Doric and Ionic orders; and as the module is lefs, all its parts will of courfe be more delicate: the fhaft may be enriched with flutings, to the number of twenty or twenty-four, as in the Ionic order; there is no reafon why they fhould be augmented. The principal members of the entablature may have the fame proportions as the two former orders, *viz.* being divided into ten equal parts, three are for the height of the architrave, three for the frize, and four for the cornice."

Having thus given the particulars relative to each order, I fhall conclude this part with fome general obfervations,

neceffary

necessary to be known and observed, in delineating or making designs in architecture; these I have extracted from the work before quoted, and have given them in the author's own words, as alteration is needless, and liable to mislead.

AN order may be divided into two parts, the column, including the plinth of its base, with the abacus of the capital; and the entablature, which includes all above the capital, and may be divided in the large, into the architrave, the frize, and the cornice.

" By examining the antiques, it will be found, that, in all their profiles, the cyma and the cavetto are constantly used as finishings, and never applied where strength is required; that the ovolo and talon are always employed as supporters to the essential members of the composition, such as the modillions, denteles, and corona; that the chief use of the torus and astragal, is to fortify the tops and bottoms of columns, and

and sometimes pedestals, where they are frequently cut in the form of ropes; and that the scotia is employed only to separate the members of bases, for which purpose the fillet is also used, notonly in bases, but in all kinds of profiles.

"An assemblage of essential parts and mouldings, is termed a profile; on the choice, disposition, and proportion of these, depends the beauty or deformity of the profile. The most perfect are, such as are composed of few mouldings, varied both in form and size, fitly applied with regard to their uses, and so disposed, that the straight and curved ones succeed each other alternately. In every profile there should be a predominant member, to which all the others ought to be subservient, and seem made either to support, to fortify, or to shelter it from the injury of the weather, as in a cornice where the corona is principal, the cyma or cavetto cover it, and the modillions, denteles, ovolo, and talon support it.

"When

" When ornaments are employed to adorn the mouldings, fome of them fhould be left plain, in order to form a proper repofe; for, when all are enriched, the figure of the profile is loft. In a cornice the corona fhould not be ornamented, nor the modillion band; neither fhould the different facias of architraves, the plinths of columns, fillets, nor fcarce any fquare member be carved; for they are, generally fpeaking, either principal in the compofition, or ufed as boundaries to other parts; in either of which cafes, their figures fhould be diftinct and unembarraffed. The dentele band fhould remain uncut, where the ovolo and talon immediately above and below it are enriched; for, when the denteles are marked, particularly if they be fmall, the three members are confounded together, and, being covered with ornament, are much too rich for the reft of the compofition; a fault carefully to be avoided, as the juft and equal diftribution of enrichments is on all occafions to be attended to.—For, in effect, the ornaments of fculpture in architecture, are like diamonds in a lady's drefs, with which it would be abfurd to cover her face, and other parts that are in themfelves beautiful."

" When mouldings of the fame form and fize are employed in one profile, they fhould be enriched with the fame kind of ornaments.—It muft be obferved, that all the ornaments of mouldings are to be regularly difpofed, and anfwering perpendicularly above each other; the middles of the modillions, denteles, oves, and other ornaments, all in a line; for nothing is more confufed and unfeemly, than to diftribute them without any kind of order. The larger parts are to regulate the fmaller; all the ornaments in the entablature are to be governed by the modillions; and thefe are to be dependent upon the intervals of the columns, and fo difpofed, that one of them may correfpond with the axis of each column.

It is farther to be observed, that the ornaments muſt partake of the character of the order which they enrich; and thoſe uſed in the Doric and Ionic orders muſt be of a ſimpler kind, and groſſer make, than thoſe employed in the Compoſite and Corinthian."

" In the exteriour, whatever does not contribute to the general effect of the whole building, is in a great meaſure uſeleſs, and an expence that might more judiciouſly be employed in places where it could be more attended to.—The parts that are in themſelves large, and ſo formed and diſpoſed as to receive broad maſſes and ſtrong impreſſions of light and ſhade, will of courſe excite great ideas; but if they are broken into a number of ſmall diviſions, and their ſurface ſo varied as to catch a thouſand impreſſions of light, demi-tint, and darkneſs, the whole will be confuſed, trifling, and incapable of cauſing any great emotions."

Thus far Sir W. Chambers. An observation or two more, and I finish the subject.

First, The appearance of columns is often varied by adding rusticated cinctures at equal (or other) distances to a column: this is a modern invention, gives a very unnatural appearance, and disguises the true figure of the pillar. Rustic work is with greater propriety, and better effect, introduced into large entrances, parks and gardens; also into grottos, baths, or fountains, where an irregular and rough appearance better suits the place and purpose.

The rule for the diminution of columns has ever varied: the ancients frequently diminished the column from the very foot, or from one quarter or one third of its height: the latter method is now generally practised: the diminution should be seldom less than one eighth part of the lower diameter of the shaft, nor more than one sixth: this latter is

the

the more graceful: fome, by way of giving a better contour or appearance, allow a fmall fwell, or bellying, in the lower part of the middle divifion of the pillar.

It may not be altogether ufelefs to give the general rules to be obferved in *pedeftals*, where it is neceffary to introduce them. A determinate rule cannot be given, as they muft vary in height according to the circumftances which render them ufeful: they have ever been confidered as mere auxiliaries, to give height, and elevate the column above furrounding objects which impede its view. When they are ufed by choice, it is common to give them one third, or one quarter part of the height of the column and entablature, which is thus divided: of nine equal parts, two are for the bafe, one for the cornice, the remaining fix for the die of the pedeftal, which is equal in fize to the plinth of the column:

the enrichments should be regulated by those of the entablature, &c.

Each column has its particular *base*. The Tuscan base is the most simple, having only a torus and plinth. The Doric base has an astragal more than the Tuscan. To the Ionic base the torus is larger on a double scotia, with two astragals between. The Corinthian base has two torus's, two scotias, and two astragals. The Composite base has one astragal less than the Corinthian. The Attic base consists of two torus's and a scotia, and is applicable to every order except the Tuscan, which has its particular base. Plate 7.

RUDIMENTS

RUDIMENTS

OF

ANCIENT ARCHITECTURE.

PART the SECOND.

OF THE TEMPLES OR SACRED BUILDINGS
OF THE ANCIENTS.

I HOPE to be pardoned in requesting the reader's attention to an observation or two, before we enter on the rules of VITRUVIUS concerning sacred buildings.

Of all the buildings of the ancients, those sacred to their Deities remain most perfect, and in the greatest number. Indeed, considering the polytheism of their religion, and how much men and nations vied in endeavouring to fhew the greateft liberality in erecting buildings to the honour of their tutelar deities, or when they had vowed worfhip and homage to any particular one; I fay, when we confider what variety of opportunities offered to fhew honour, to exhibit fplendour, and to difplay liberality, we need not wonder at the great number of facred edifices ftill remaining: indeed they are fo many, and of fuch magnificence, as chiefly to abforb the traveller's attention, the remains of other public ftructures being but few. I have therefore given no more on public edifices, than what VITRUVIUS has written of facred ones, and the rules given by him for the difpofition of columns.

OF TEMPLES.

THE following account of their origin and progrefs will, I think, be confidered as rational; for doubtlefs they had
their

their states of progression, as well as every other human invention.

Nature has implanted in the mind of man so strong an idea of a superior power, that every nation has some worship or ceremonies, by which they shew their dependance on, and reverence of, a Deity, whose purity of nature requires distinct places for religious services, attended by every mark of awe and respect, best suited to express their ideas of reverence and submission to Omnipotent Power.

As mankind in the rudest state ever acknowledged Powers Divine, the places best calculated to inspire religious ideas were groves, or thick woody places, where gloomy dulness and shade naturally impress the mind with awe, and lead it to contemplation. Such, we may therefore suppose, were the places first set apart for religious worship; but when the weather, or inclination, rendered an enclosed place desirable, they laboured, in this early state of arts, to produce a

building

building merely fuited to the neceffary purpofes. But when fociety was more enlarged and refined, and the profits of commerce accumulated to wealth, then the mind of man, which naturally runs toward excellence, was not content with the plain and fimple ftructures already built: and, it is likely no fmall fpur was alfo ufed by the influence of thofe concerned in the worfhip and facrifices of the times; for additional wealth naturally excited an increafe of fplendour and more coftly ceremonies: thefe required more room, and a correfponding increafe of ftate and magnificence, that the feveral rites, &c. might be fuitably performed: thus, an edifice of more elegance, a building of greater extent and richer embellifhments was required, which would fhew fuperiour honour and refpect to the Deity worfhipped.

THUS, from the fimpleft ftructure, rofe the Antis, Proftyle, &c. till invention and ingenuity, aided by unbounded liberality,

berality, crowned the whole with the hypæthral edifice. Excited by ambition, and enabled by vaft riches, whofe fources were far extended territory and numerous fertile provinces, emperors, and even private perfons, were enabled to erect the moft coftly temples, the extent and magnificence of which are truly aftonifhing.

It is a remark worthy notice, that the ancient architects did not follow in a fervile manner the rules delivered by Vitruvius: yet certainly what he wrote, were the rules by which they planned their great outline, or defign; however they might vary the fmaller or inferior parts of an edifice. To enumerate a few inftances of variation:

The Temple of Minerva at Athens has eight columns in front; and Vitruvius allows but fix to a peripteral, of which order this building is.

The Temple of Minerva Pollias has fix columns in front, yet is proftyle; although

although Vitruvius allows but four to this order.

The Temple of Jupiter Olympus at Athens has no more than eight columns in front, yet is hypæthral, to which Vitruvius gives ten columns in front. This is a variation recorded by himfelf, and without any particular notice of the violation of the rule ; from which it fhould appear as not confide#ed of much confequence.

The walls of the cell were always placed oppofite the columns of the pronaos, and pofticum, according to the rule; at leaft I recollect but one example to the contrary, which is in the Temple of Thefeus at Athens.—I thought it neceffary to notice thefe inftances of the variation of the ancient architects, that the refearches and genius of modern times might not be led into error, or fettered by obferving as law, that which was not adhered to by thofe we wifh to imitate.

VITRUVIUS

VITRUVIUS

on

SACRED BUILDINGS.

" SACRED Buildings, or Temples, differ in their various figures and aspects. Of the first order is the *Antis*. 2*dly*, The *Proftyle*. 3*dly*, The *Amphiproftyle*. 4*thly*, The *Peripteral*. 5*thly*, The *Pfeudodipteral*. 6*thly*, The *Dipteral*. 7*thly*, The *Hypæthral*, which are distinguished in this manner.

THE edifice or temple is called *Antiæ*, when it has in the front antæ, or pilasters, at the corners of the wall which forms the cell; and between the pilasters in the middle, two columns, which support the pediment or porch; of which examples are at the three Temples of Fortune, the one neareft the Colline Gate.

2*dly*, The *Proftyle* is the fame as the Antis, only columns are placed oppofite the pilafters of each corner, which fupport a chapiter or architrave, the fame as in the Antis: an example of this manner is the Temple of Jupiter and Faunus, in the Ifle of Tyber.

3*dly*, The *Amphiproftyle* is the fame as the preceding, only a poftern or back front *(Pofticum)* is added, with columns and pediment, the fame as to the Proftyle.

4*thly*, The *Peripteral* has in the front and hinder porch *(Pofticum)* fix columns, and eleven, counting the corner ones, on each fide. And thefe columns are fo placed, that the fpace of an intercolumniation fhall be left between the wall and the outer range of columns, leaving an ambulatory round the cell of the edifice: as in the Gate of Metellus, the Temple of Jupiter Stator defigned by Hermodius; and that founded by Mariana to Honour

and

and Virtue, built by Mutius, and wants the hinder porch.

5thly, To the *Pseudodipteral*, the columns are so placed, that in the front and behind there are eight columns, and on each side, counting the corner ones, fifteen; and the walls of the cell must correspond, or run parallel with the four centre columns, both before and behind: there must be the space of two intercolumniations, and the thickness of one column between the walls and the outer columns. Of this order Rome affords no example; but at Magnesia, the Temple of Diana, by Hermogines Alabandin; and that of Apollo, built by Amnesta, are examples.

6thly, THE *Dipteral* is octostyle or eight-columned, both before and behind; but it has a double row of columns round the cell, as in the Temple of Jupiter Quirinus of the Doric order, and the Ionic Temple of Diana at Ephesus, built by Ctesiphon.

7thly, THE *Hypæthral* is decastyle or

ten-columned, both before and behind: the other parts are the fame as the Dipteral, but within it has a double row of columns, one above the other all round, refembling a porch, which is called a Periftyle: the middle has no roof; it has folding-doors both before and behind. We have no example of this at Rome; but Athens has one, the Temple of Jupiter Olympus, which is octoftyle or eight-columned.

THERE are alfo round temples, of which fome are *Monopteral*, without cells, and built on columns: the other is called *Peripteral*. Thofe without cells have a tribunal or throne, and are afcended by fteps of one third of the diameter of the temple: the columns, placed on pedeftals, are as high as the diameter of the temple, taken at the outer fide of the pedeftals; their thicknefs is one tenth part of the height of the fhaft and capital: the height of the architrave is half the diameter of the column: the frize, and other ornaments

ments above, may be according to the general rule.

THE *Peripteral* is built with an afcent of two fteps, on which the pedeftals of the columns are placed: the wall of the cell is diftant one fifth part of the diameter of the temple from the pedeftals of the columns: in the middle is left a fpace for folding doors: the diameter of the inner part of the cell muft be equal to the height of a column without the pedeftal; the columns round the cell are placed with fuitable proportion and fymmetry. The enclofure in the middle is thus proportioned: one diameter of the whole building for its height; half is for the cupola, exclufive of a flower on the top of the pyramid: the fize of the flower fhall be the fame as a capital of the columns; the other parts may be according to the proportions already written.

BY the fame general proportions other kind of temples are built, but have different difpofitions of their parts; as the temple

ple of Caftor in the Circus of Flaminius: and the temple of Vejovius between the two groves; alfo the temple of Diana of the Groves; where the columns are added on both fides the walls of the porch. This kind of building, as in the temple of Caftor in the Circus, was firft ufed in the temple of Minerva within the citadel at Athens, and in the temple of Pallas at Sunium in Attica. They have the fame proportions as the others; for the cell is in length double its breadth; and the fame rule is followed for the fides as for the fronts.

Some there are who ufe the Tufcan difpofition of the columns, although they are of the Corinthian or Ionic orders.

To temples, whofe walls with the antæ project to form a porch, two columns are placed oppofite the walls which form the cell; thus blending the Tufcan and Greek manners.

Again, others by removing the walls of the cell, and placing them between

the

the intercolumniation, leave a very large fpace within the cell; the other parts preferve the fame proportion and fymmetry. Thus has arifen a new order, which is called *Pfeudodipteral*; and this kind is particularly ufeful for facrifices. The fame kind of temple cannot be made to every god, becaufe of the diverfity of the ceremonies to be performed.

Thus I have explained, as far as I was able, every kind of facred building—their order—the fymmetry of their parts—the difference of their figure; and what variety is to be obferved in them, I have been careful in writing."

The elegance and magnificence of a ftructure depending very much on the proper placing of the columns; and as it appears connected with the fubject here treated of, I add the rules laid down by Vitruvius, obferved by the ancients, and allowed by the moderns, in the difpofition of columns, called by that writer

THE FIVE SPECIES OF BUILDING.

" OF buildings there are five forts or species; which are called, 1ft, The *Pycnoftyle*, that is, thick of columns. 2d, The *Syftyle*, that are a little wider. 3d, The *Diaftyle*, ftill wider. 4th, The *Araeoftyle*, more diftant than is proper. 5th, The *Euftyle*, which is the proper diftance.

To the *Pycnoftyle*, the diftance of the intercolumniation is one diameter and a half of the column; as in the temple of the divine Julius; the temple of Venus in Cæfar's Forum; and many others after the fame manner.

THE *Syftyle* has two diameters of the column between the intercolumniation, and the plinths of the bafe are equal to the fpace which is between two plinths; as in the temple of Fortuna Equeftris, near the Stone Theatre, and others made after

after the fame proportions. Both thefe forts are inconvenient; for the ladies, when entering the temple to worfhip, cannot pafs the columns arm in arm unlefs they go fide-ways: alfo, by the frequency of the columns, the view of the door, and the figns or trophies of the deity, are hid, and the narrownefs of the porch is inconvenient for walking.

The *Dyaftyle* has this diftribution, viz. three diameters of the columns between the intercolumniations, as in the temple of Apollo and Diana. This has its inconveniencies; becaufe the architrave, on account of the diftance between the column, is liable to break.

In the *Aræoftyle* they ufe neither ftone nor marble, but make the beams of durable timber. This kind of building is ftraggling and heavy, low and broad. The pinacles are generally ornamented with fictile or earthen ware, or brafs gilt after the Tufcan manner, as is to be feen in the Circus Maximus at the Temple of Ceres,

Ceres, and in Pompey's Temple of Hercules, and alfo in the Capitol.

THE *Euftyle* manner is now to be treated of; which, with great juftice, for its ufefulnefs, beauty, and durability, merits every commendation. It is formed by allowing to the diftance of the intercolumniations two diameters and a quarter, and to the middle intercolumniation only, both before and behind, three diameters. Thus the figure has a beautiful afpect, is acceffible without impediment; and round the cell is a ftately ambulatory.

THE rule is this:

THE front of the building of it is *Tetraftyle* (four columns), is divided into eleven parts and a half, without reckoning the projection of the bafe of the column. If it is *Hexaftyle* (fix columns), it is divided into eighteen parts. If it is *Octaftyle* (eight columns), it is divided into twenty-four parts and a half. Of thefe parts one, whether the building be tetraftyle, hexaftyle, or octaftyle, fhall be a module, which is

to

to be the thickneſs of a column. Each intercolumniation, except the middle one, muſt be two modules and a quarter; the middle one ſhall have three modules both before and behind: the height of the columns ſhall be eight modules and a half: by this diviſion of the intercolumniation, the columns have a juſt proportion. Rome affords no example of this kind; but at Teos in Aſia is one, the temple of Bacchus, which is octaſtyle.

HERMOGENES was the firſt inventor of theſe proportions; he alſo firſt uſed the octaſtyle pſeudodipteral: he firſt contrived to take away, without injuring the beauty, the interior range of columns in the dipteral (which are thirty-four), thereby very much decreaſing both the labour and expence: this alſo gave a very large ambulatory round the cell, and, without miſſing the ſuperfluity, preſerved the majeſty of the whole; for the walls and the columns were firſt thus diſpoſed, that the view, on account of the afperity *(afperitas)* of the intercolumniation, fhould have more majefty: befides, it has this convenience, of fheltering a great many perfons from rain, as well round as within the cell, which includes a great fpace. This difpofition of pfeudodipteral buildings, was firft difcovered by the labour of the great and difcerning fpirit of Hermogenes; which, like a fountain, will ferve pofterity from whence to draw rules for the Science of Architecture.

THE columns to the *Aræoftyle* fhould have for their thicknefs one eighth part of their height. For the *Diaftyle*, the height of the column is to be divided into eight parts and a half; one part for the thicknefs of the column. For the *Syftyle*, the height fhall be divided into nine parts and a half; one part for the thicknefs of the column. Alfo for the *Pycnoftyle*, the height fhall be divided into ten parts; one part for the thicknefs of the column. The *Euftyle* alfo is divided

into

into eight parts and a half, the fame as the Diaftyle: one part is given for the thicknefs of the column; and for the folidity of its parts it fhall have its proper intercolumniation. As the fpace between the columns increafes, fo ought alfo the thicknefs of the columns. If it is aræoftyle, and they fhould have only a ninth or tenth part for their thicknefs, they will then appear tall and flender, on account of the length of the intervals; for the air will in appearance diminifh the thicknefs of the columns. On the contrary, if it is pycnoftyle, and the columns have an eighth part for their thicknefs, they have a clumfy and ungraceful appearance, on account of the frequency of the columns, and the narrownefs of the intervals: for this reafon, the fymmetry and proportion of each order fhould be attended to. Alfo the thicknefs of the corner columns muft be increafed one fiftieth part; for, by the great furrounding fpace, they will appear fmaller to the

view,

view, and it is neceffary art fhould rectify this defect of vifion.

For the diminution of the fhaft of a column, the following rule may be obferved: if the fhaft of a column is fifteen feet high, the diameter of the lower part is divided into fix parts; five of which are for the top diameter. If columns are from fifteen to twenty feet high, the lower diameter is divided into fix parts and a half; five and a half of which are for the top diameter. If columns are from twenty to thirty feet high, the lower diameter is divided into feven parts; fix of which are for the top diameter. If columns are from thirty to forty feet high, the lower diameter is divided into feven parts and a half; fix and a half of which are for the top diameter. If columns are from forty to fifty feet high, the lower diameter is divided into eight parts; feven of which are for the top diameter. If any are higher than thofe mentioned, they

they shall have the same proportions for their diminution.—An additional thickness is properly given, on account of the increased height; for, as the eye is attracted by beauty, it is necessary it should be flattered by the pleasure it receives from proportionate and just distribution of parts, as it is when deceived by judicious additions; else the whole will have a bulky and inelegant effect."

A

DICTIONARY of TERMS

USED IN

ARCHITECTURE.

DICTIONARY.

A.

ABACUS, the upper member of a column, which serves as a covering to the capital; to the Tuscan, Doric and Ionic, is square; to the modern Ionic, Corinthian and Composite, each side is arched or cut inwards, and is decorated in the centre with a flower or other ornament. See plates 9, 10.

ACANTHUS, a plant, whose leaves form an ornament in the Corinthian and Composite capitals, and are said to have originally given rise to the former order.

ACROTERIA, a kind of base, placed on the angles of pediments, usually for the support of statues, &c.

AMPHIPROSTYLE, *i. e.* double prostyle, or having pillars on both fronts; according to Vitruvius, the third order of temples. See page 46.

AMPHITHEATRE, a place for exhibiting fhows, very fpacious, of a round or oval figure, with many feats rifing on every fide.

ANNULET, a fmall fquare moulding, which ferves to crown or accompany a larger, and to feparate the flutings in columns. See plate 8.

ANTÆ, a fpecies of pilafters on the extremity of a wall, ufually have no diminution, nor do the mouldings of their capitals or bafes always refemble thofe of the columns.

ANTÆ or *Antis*, i. e. pilafteral; according to Vitruvius, the firft order of temples. See page 45.

APOPHYGE, that part of a column where it begins to rife upwards out of its bafe.

AQUÆDUCT, an artificial canal, built for the conveyance of water from one place to another, either running under ground, or rifing above it.

ARCH, part of a circle or ellipfis.

ARÆOSTYLE, according to Vitruvius, the fourth method or fpecies of intercolumniation,

niation, to which four diameters are allowed between each column. See page 53.

ARCHITRAVE, the lowest principal member of an entablature, lying immediately upon the abacus of the capital. See plates 9, 10.

ASTRAGAL, a small round member resembling a ring, which terminates the extremities of the column; is sometimes used to divide the facia of the architrave, when it is frequently cut into beads, &c. See plate 8.

ATTIC BASE. See *Base*. See plate 7.

B.

BALUSTER, small columns, or pillars of wood, stone, &c. used on terraces or tops of buildings for ornament, and to support railing, and when continued form a *baluſtrade*.

BAND, a general term for a low, flat, or square member.

BASE, the lower and projecting part of a column and pedestal. See page 38. See plates 7, 10.

BASILIC, a royal palace; among the ancients was a great hall, with a portico, isles, tribunal, &c. where the king in person distributed justice; it is also applied to modern

modern churches when fpacious and elegant.

Bossage, a term ufed for any ftone laid with a projection beyond the upright of a building, to be afterwards cut into mouldings or other ornaments; it is alfo ufed for ruftic work, becaufe the ruftics project over the perpendicular of the building.

Butment, fupporters or props, on or againft which the feet of arches reft.

Buttress, a kind of butment, built fometimes archwife, as to Gothic buildings; a mafs of ftone or brick work, ferving to prop or fupport buildings, walls, &c. on the outfide, where their great height or weight require additional ftrength.

C.

Caliducts, pipes or canals, difpofed in or along the walls of houfes, for conveying hot air to diftant apartments, from a common or centrical furnace, as practifed by the ancients.—This method has been adapted in modern buildings with good fuccefs and œconomy.

Capital, the uppermoft member of a column, which is as a crown or head thereto,

thereto, placed immediately over the *shaft*, and under the *architrave*; no column is complete without a capital, which is a distinguishing mark of each order.— Tuscan and Doric capitals consist of mouldings; Ionic, Corinthian, and Composite capitals, of leaves and other ornaments.

CARTOUCHE, an ornament in sculpture representing a scroll of paper, &c.

CARYATIDES, a kind of order in Architecture, in which a female figure is applied instead of a pillar; the origin of which is thus handed down by Vitruvius. The inhabitants of Caria, a city of Peloponnesus, made a league with the Persians against their own nation; but the Persians being worsted, they were afterwards besieged by the victorious party, their city taken and reduced to ashes, the men put to the sword, and the women carried away captives. To perpetuate the memory of this victory, the conquerors caused public edifices to be erected, in which, as a mark of degradation and servility, the figures of the captives were used instead of columns, thus handing to pofterity their merited fervility and pu-nifhment. When figures of the male fex are ufed, they are called *Perfians* or *Perfes*.

CATADROME, an engine of the ancients, like a crane, ufed to raife great weights.

CAVETTO, a concave moulding of one quarter of a circle. See plate 8.

CAULICOLI, the little twifts or volutes under the flower on the abacus in the Corinthian capital, reprefent the twifted tops of the acanthus ftalks; are called alfo *Helices*.

CELL, in an ancient temple, is the inclofed fpace within the walls.

CINCTURE, a ring, lift, or fillet, at the top and bottom of the fhaft of the column; that at the bottom is called *Apophyge*; the top one is called *Annulet*, or *Aftragal*.

COLLARIN, or *Collarino*, the neck or frize of a Tufcan or Doric capital.

COLONNADE, a feries or continuation of columns.

COLUMN, a round pillar ufed in Architecture, to adorn or fupport. Columns are of five kinds; the *Tufcan*, *Doric*, *Ionic*, *Corinthian*, and *Compofite*, each of which
has

has its particular proportion. The term includes the base and the capital.

COMPOSITE *order*, one of the five orders of Architecture.

CONGE, a small moulding, which serves to separate larger ones, called also *List* or *Annulet*.

CONSOLE, an ornament cut on the key-stone of arches, with a projection, capable of supporting busts, vases, &c.

CONTOUR, the outline of a figure, or piece of Architecture.

COPING *of a wall*, the top or covering made sloping to throw off water.

CORBEILLE, carved work, representing a basket with fruits or flowers, serving as a finish to some other ornament. It sometimes is applied to the vase of the Corinthian capital, the word originally meaning a basket.

CORINTHIAN *order*, one of the five orders of Architecture.

CORNICE, the upper assemblage of members in an entablature, commencing at the frize; each order has its particular cornice, with suitable enrichments. To the

Tuscan it is quite plain; to the *Doric* are added *guttæ*, or bells in the *soffit*: the *Ionic* has plain modillions; the *Corinthian* is much enriched, and has modillions; the *Composite* is not quite so much enriched as the Corinthian. See plates 9, 10.

CORONA, a large flat and strong member in a cornice, called also the *Drip*, or *Larmier*; its use is to screen the under parts of the work, and, from its shape, to prevent the water running down the column; it has always a large projection to answer its proposed use. The under, or horizontal part of the corona, is called the *Soffit*, and admits of various degrees of ornament, according to the richness of the order.

CORRIDOR, a gallery or passage in large buildings, which leads to distant apartments.

CRYPTO-PORTICUS, a vaulted, subterraneous, or obscure place; also the decorations at the entrance of a grotto.

CUPOLA, a round roof or dome, in the form of an inverted cup.

CYMA, *Cima*, or *Cymatium*, a species of moulding,

ing, which is generally the upper one to an entablature. There are two forts of this moulding, the *cyma recta*, and *cyma reversa*. See plate 8.

D.

DECASTYLE, in ancient Architecture, a building, with ten columns in front.

DENTELE, an ornament resembling teeth, used in Ionic and Corinthian cornices.

DIASTYLE, according to Vitruvius, the third species of intercolumniation, having three diameters between the columns.

DIE, the square or naked piece in a pedestal, that part which is between the base and the capital. See plate 10.

DIPTEROS, *i. e.* having a double range of columns; according to the arrangement of Vitruvius, is the sixth order of temples.

DOME, a spherical roof.—See *Cupola*.

DORIC *order*, one of the five orders of Architecture.

DRIP. See *Corona*.

DROPS or *Guttæ*, in the Doric entablature, are small pyramids or cones, immediately under the triglyph.

E.

ECHINUS, is properly the egg and anchor ornament peculiar to the *Ionic* capital; it is sometimes used for the whole member instead of *ovolo*.

ENCARPUS, used to express festoons of fruits or flowers on frizes, &c. Literally means fruit only.

ENTABLATURE, an ornament or assemblage of parts, supported by a column or pilaster over the capital: each order of columns has a peculiar entablature divided into three principal parts; the *architrave*, which is divided into two or more *facias*, and rests upon the capital. The *frize* is next, and may be plain or ornamented. The *cornice* is the top or crowning part. See plates 9, 10.

EPISTYLE, the same as architrave.

EUSTYLE, according to Vitruvius, the fifth and most eligible method of intercolumniation, having two diameters and a quarter between the columns.

EXHEDRA, in ancient Architecture, a large recess, where company used to retire for conversation, &c. in some buildings was a distinct apartment.

FAÇADE,

F.

FAÇADE, the front view or elevation of a building.

FACIA, a flat member in the entablature of an order, reprefenting a band or broad fillet in an architrave; if divided, thefe divifions are called the firft facia, the fecond facia, &c. See plate 9.

FASTIGIUM, the name ufed by Vitruvius for what we call a *Pediment*.

FILLET. See *Annulet*.

FLUTINGS, the hollows or channels, which are cut perpendicularly in columns by way of ornament.

FOLIAGE, an affemblage of leaves.

FRIZE, the middle member of an entablature, having the architrave below, and the cornice above.

FRONTISPIECE, fometimes fignifies the whole face or afpect of a building, but is more properly applied to the decorated entrance of a houfe.

FUST, the fhaft of a column, or that part which is between the bafe and the capital.

GLYPHS,

G.

GLYPHS, the perpendicular channels cut in the *triglyphs* of the Doric frize.

GOLA, or *Gula*, a moulding, more ufually called *cyma reverfa*, or *ogee*.

GORGE, a hollow moulding, a *cavetto*.

GOTHIC, a peculiar ftyle of Architecture, diftinct from the Grecian or Roman, derived from the Goths, or rather from the Saracens.

GULA. See *Gola*.

GUTTÆ. See *Drops*.

H.

HELIX, or *Helices*. See Cauliculi.

HEXASTYLE, a place having fix columns in front.

HIPPODROME, a place where the ancients exercifed their horfes, alfo the courfe for the horfe-race.

HOUSE, the houfes of the ancients had great and magnificent veftibules or entries, which were fometimes two hundred and twenty feet long, and one hundred and fixty broad, fupported with two ranges of pillars, which formed a wing on each fide.

The

The Greeks and the Romans differed in the diftributing and ordering their apartments. The Romans had magnificent courts and entries, but the Greeks only a narrow entry through which they paffed into a periftyle; this entry or paffage had on one fide the porter's lodge, and on the other the ftables. Among the Greeks, the apartments of the women were feparate from thofe of the men, and the latter dined by themfelves.

THE ancients had three forts of *halls* or *veftibules*, viz. the *Corinthian*, which had pillars round againft the wall; thefe fupported the ceiling which was vaulted : the fecond was the *Egyptian* hall; in this the pillars were detached from the wall in the manner of a *periftyle*. The fpace between the columns and the wall was covered with a pavement, and formed a walk or balcony round. The range of pillars fupported an architrave, on which was another range of columns, between which were the windows. The third was the *Cyzican* hall, which was ufed chiefly by the Greeks, and had this in particular, that they faced
the

the North, and had a profpect of the garden.

HYPÆTHRAL, *i. e.* uncovered, or open to the fky; according to Vitruvius, the feventh order of temples, and without a roof.

HYPOTRACHELION, the neck or frize of a capital.

I.

IMPOST, a facia or fmall cornice which crowns a pier or pilafter, and from which an arch fprings.

INSULATED, ftanding alone, or detached from any contiguous buildings, &c.

INTERCOLUMNIATION, the fpace between two columns, for the particulars of which, fee page 52.

IONIC *order*, one of the five orders of Architecture.

K.

KEY-STONE, the higheft ftone of an arch, to which a projection is ufually given, and fometimes cut in ornaments.

L.

LARMIER. See *Corona.*
LIST, or *Liftel.* See *Annulet.*

METOPE,

M.

METOPE, the interval or square space between the triglyphs in the Doric frize.

MEZZANINE, or *Mezzetti*, small or low stories between principal ones, used as servants apartments.

MINUTE, an *architectonic measure*, the lower diameter of a column divided into sixty parts, each part is a *minute*.

MODILLION, an ornament resembling a bracket, in the Ionic, Corinthian, and Composite cornices. See plate 9.

MODULE, an *architectonic measure*, the lower diameter of a column divided into two parts, one is a *module*, each module is divided into thirty *minutes*; thus either is not a determinate, but a proportionate measure.

MONOPTERAL, a round temple without a cell. See page 48.

MOULDINGS, those parts which project beyond the base or perpendicular face of a wall, column, &c. intended only for ornament, whether round, flat, or curved: the regular mouldings are, 1st, the *list* or *annulet*; 2d, the *astragal* or *bead*; 3d, the *cyma reversa*, or ogee; 4th, the

cyma

cyma recta; 5th, the *cavetto*, or hollow; 6th, the *ovolo* or quarter round; 7th, the *scotia*; 8th, the *torus*. See plate 8. For general obfervations on mouldings, their difpofition, &c. fee page 32.

MUTULE, an ornament in the Doric cornice, anfwering to a *modillion* in the Ionic and Corinthian entablatures.

N.

NICHE, a cavity or hollow in a wall for ftatues, &c.

O.

OCTASTYLE, an edifice having eight columns in front.

OGEE, a *cyma reverfa*.

ORDER, in Architecture, a column entire, confifting of *bafe*, *fhaft*, and *capital*, with an *entablature*. For a particular account of each *order*, fee the beginning of this work.

OVA, or *ovum*. See *Echinus*.

OVOLO, a moulding which projects one quarter of a circle, called alfo a *quarter round*. See plate 8.

PEDESTAL,

P.

PEDESTAL, a fquare body on which columns, &c. are placed. See plate 10.

PEDIMENT, a low triangular ornament in the front of buildings, and over doors, windows, &c.

PIER, a kind of pilafter or buttrefs, to fupport, ftrengthen, or ornament; the pier of a bridge, is the foot or fupport of the arch; the wall between windows or doors. Alfo fquare pillars of ftone or brick, to which gates to an entrance are hung.

PENTASTYLE, an edifice having five columns in front.

PERIDROME, the fpace in a *Peripteral* temple, which is between the column and the cell.

PERIPTERAL, *i.e.* having columns all around; according to Vitruvius, the fourth order of temple; alfo around temples.

PERISTYLE, a range of columns or colonnade, with a court or building like a cloifter: the internal colonnade to the *Hypæthral* temple, is a *periftyle*.

PIAZZA, a continued arched way or vaulting, under which to walk, &c.

PILASTER, a square pillar or column, usually placed against a wall; has the same proportions and ornaments as a column.

PILLAR, this word is generally used in Architecture, in common with *column*, though strictly speaking they are different; thus the supporters in Gothic Architecture are pillars, but can never be properly termed columns, varying in shape and every particular from the latter.

PLAT-BAND, any flat square moulding with little projection; the different facias of an architrave are called plat-bands; the same is applied to the list between flutings, &c.

PLINTH, the lower member of a base. See plates 9, 10.

PORCH, an arched way, or covering at the entrance of a great building, particularly to churches.

PORTICO, a continued range of columns covered at top, to shelter from the weather; among the ancients these were highly ornamented, and of great extent. The remains of the portico at Palmyra show it to have been full four thousand feet long.

POSTICUM,

POSTICUM, the porch in the back front of an ancient temple.

PROFILE, the outline or contour of any building, &c.

PROSTYLE, *i. e.* having pillars in front only; according to Vitruvius, the second order of temples.

PRONAOS, the front porch of an ancient temple.

PSEUDO-DIPTERAL, *i. e.* false or imperfect dipteral, the inner range of columns being omitted; according to Vitruvius, the fifth order of temples.

PYCNOSTYLE, according to Vitruvius, the first method of intercolumniation, having one diameter and a half between each column.

PYRAMID, a structure, which, from a square, triangular or other base, rises gradually to a point.

Q.

QUARTER ROUND, a moulding. See *Ovolo*.

QUOINS, stones or other materials put in the angles of buildings to strengthen them.

R.

RELIEVO, signifies the projection of any carved ornament.

ROMAN *order*, the fame as the *Compofite*.

ROTUNDA, a building which is round both within and without.

RUSTIC, the term is applied to thofe ftones in a building which are hatched or picked in holes, refembling a natural rough appearance.

S.

SALOON, a lofty, vaulted, fpacious hall or apartment.

SCAPUS, the fhaft of a column.

SCIMA. See *cyma*.

SCOTIA, a hollow moulding ufed in bafes to capitals. See plate 8.

SECTION of a building, reprefents it as if cut perpendicularly from the roof downwards, and ferves to fhew the internal decorations and diftribution.

SHAFT, the trunk or body of a column between the bafe and the capital.

SOFFIT, the under part or ceiling of a cornice, which is ufually ornamented; the under part of the *corona* is called the *Soffit*; the word is alfo applied to the ceiling of an arch, the under fide of an architrave, &c.

STOA,

STOA, a *portico*.

STYLOBATUM, the pedestal of a column.

SYSTYLE, according to Vitruvius, the second method of intercolumniation, having two diameters between the columns.

T.

TAILLOIR, the *abacus*.

TALON, a *cyma reversa*.

TEMPLE, among the ancients, according to Vitruvius, there were seven different kinds or orders, see page 45. The word is applied to buildings used to decorate modern gardens, &c.

TENIA, the upper member of the Doric architrave, a kind of *listel*.

TETRASTYLE, a building with four columns in front.

TONDINO, an *astragal*.

TORUS, or *Tore*, a large semicircular moulding, used in the base of columns. See plate 8.

TRABEATION, the entablature.

TRIGLYPH, an ornament peculiar to the Doric frize. See plate 10.

TROCHILUS, the *scotia*.

TUSCAN *order*, one of the five orders of Architecture.

TYMPAN, the flat surface or space within a pediment.

V.

VASE, the body of a Corinthian capital, also an ornament used in Architecture, &c.

VAULT, an arched roof, the stones or materials of which are so placed as to support each other.

VESTIBULE, the hall or entrance within large houses.

VOLUTE, the scroll or spiral horn, used in Ionic and Composite capitals.

X.

XYST, a large court with a portico on three sides, planted with rows of trees, where the ancients performed athletic exercises—running, wrestling, &c.

Z.

ZOCLE, or *Zoccolo*, a low square member, which serves to elevate a statue, vase, &c. also when a range of columns is erected on one continued high *plinth*, it is called a *Zocle*; it differs from a pedestal, being without base or cornice.

F I N I S.

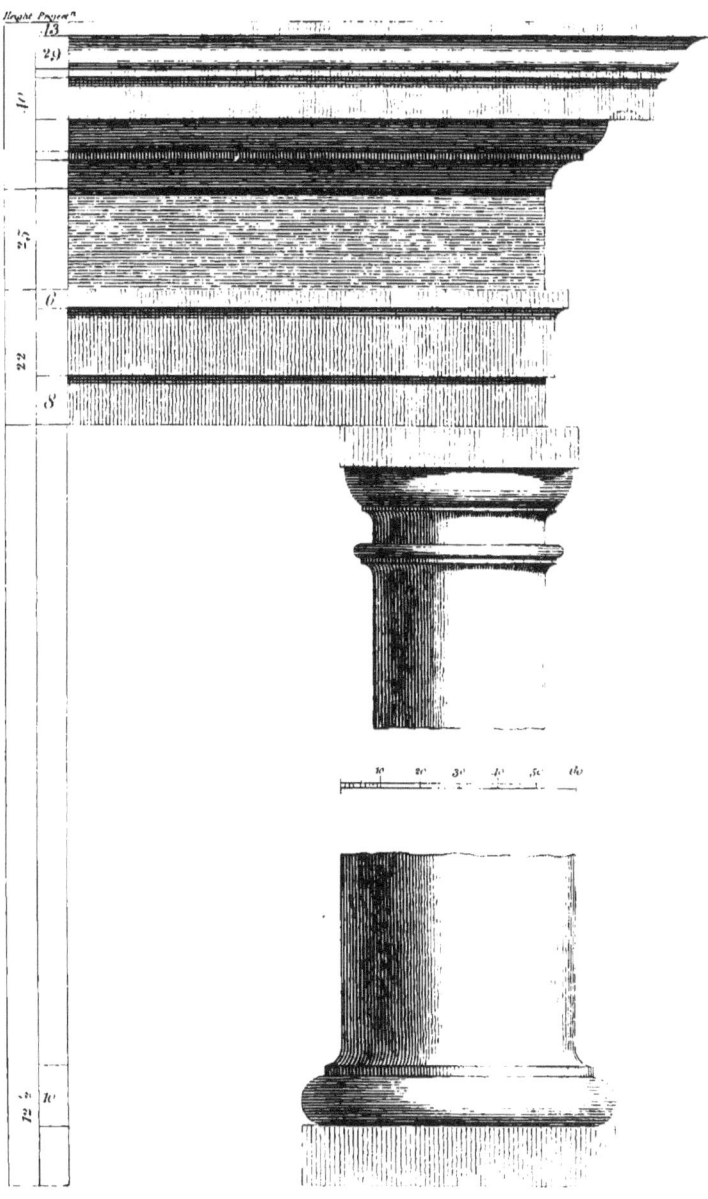

DORIC.

Plate 3

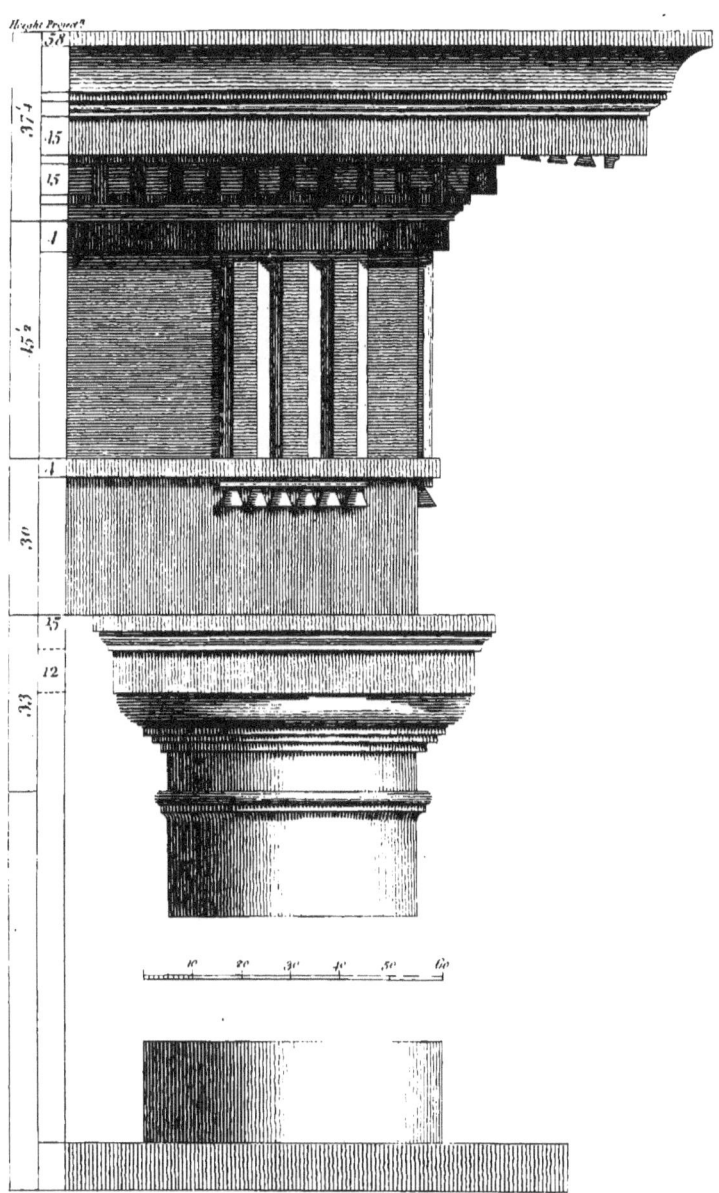

London Printed for I. & J. Taylor, at the Architectural Library, Holborn.

IONIC.

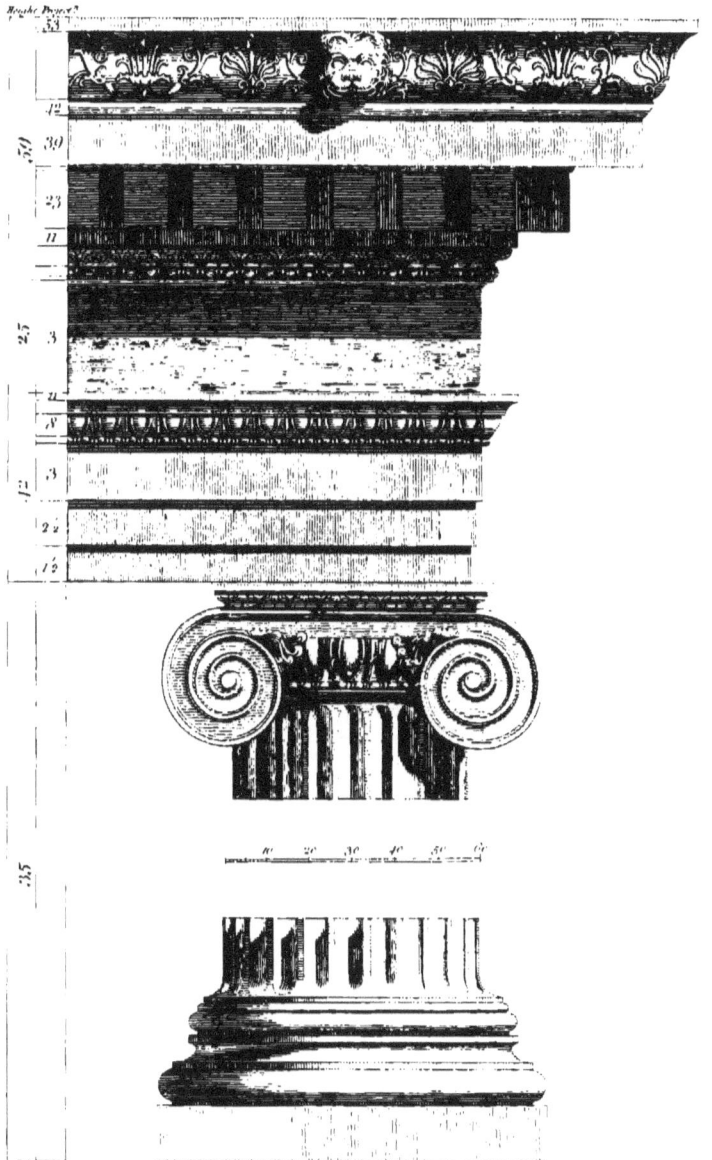

CORINTHIAN.

COMPOSITE.

London Printed for I & J Taylor at the Architectural Library, Holborn

BASES.

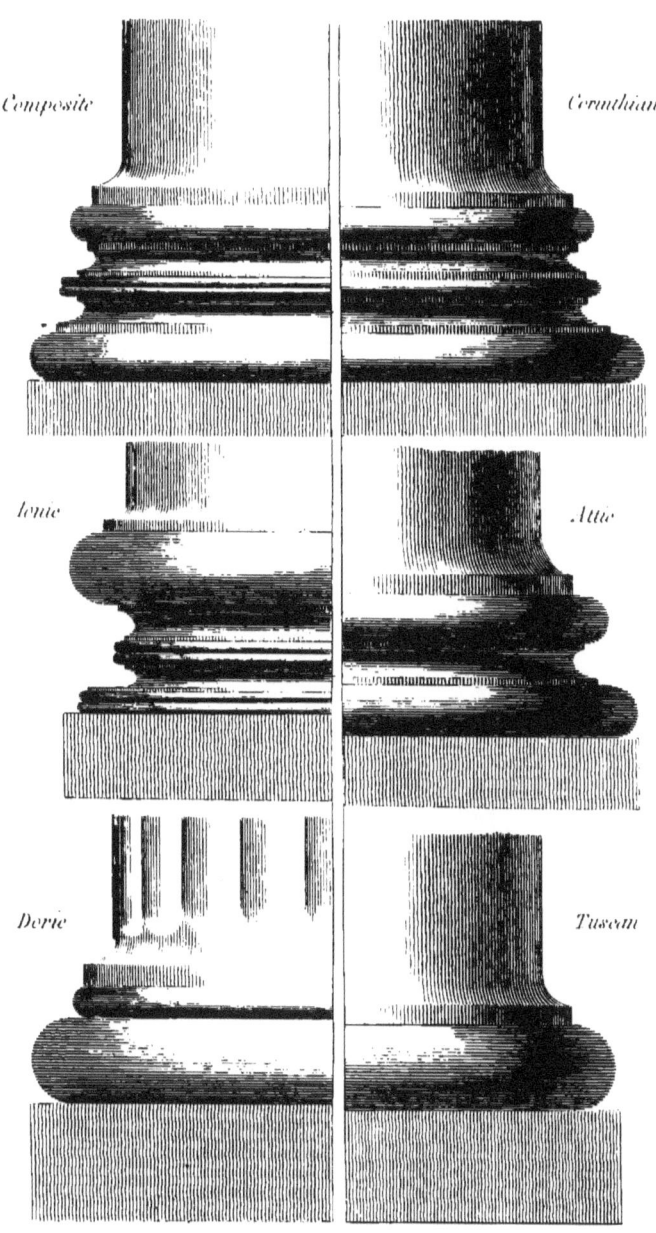

London. Printed for J. & J. Taylor, at the Architectural Library, Holborn.

MOULDINGS.

Annulet, List or Square.

Astragal or Bead.

Cima reversa or Ogee.

Cima recta.

Cavetto or hollow.

Ovolo or Quarter round.

Scotia.

Torus.

London Printed for I.&J. Taylor at the Architectural Library Holborn.

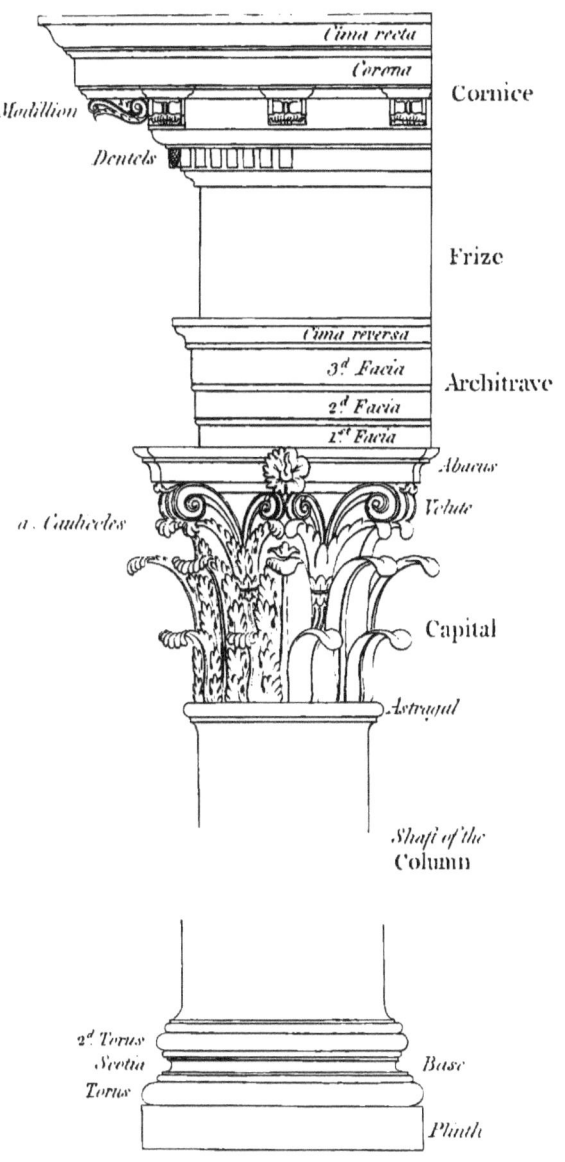

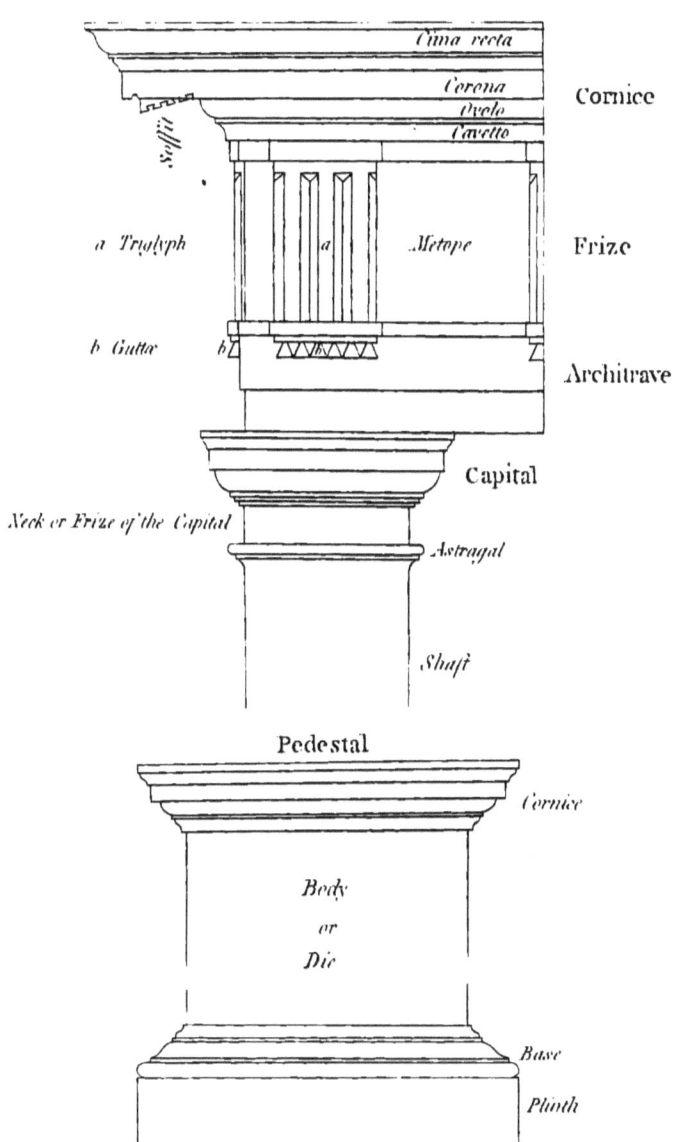

A CATALOGUE OF

Modern Books on Architecture, &c.

THEORETICAL, PRACTICAL, and ORNAMENTAL;

Which, with the beft Ancient Authors, are conftantly on Sale

AT

I. and J. TAYLOR's Architectural Library,

No. 56, *High Holborn, London.*

1. *THE Rudiments of Ancient Architecture*; in two Parts: containing an Hiftorical Account of the Five Orders, with their Proportion, and Examples of each from the Antiques: Alfo, *Vitruvius* on the Temples and Intercolumniations, &c. of the Ancients, calculated for the Ufe of thofe who wifh to attain a fummary Knowledge of the Science of Architecture; with a Dictionary of Terms: illuftrated with ten Plates, and a Portrait of the celebrated *James Stuart*, Efq. Price, in boards, 5s.

2. Plans, Elevations. and Sections, of Buildings, executed in the counties of *Norfolk, Suffolk, Yorkfhire, Wiltfhire, Warwickfhire, Staffordfhire, Somerfetfhire*, &c. By *J hn Soane*, Architect, Member of the Royal Academies of P rma and Florence. Dedicated, with permiffion, to the King. On Forty-feven folio Plates. Price, on Royal Paper, 2l. 2s. on Imperial Paper, 2l. 12s. 6d.

3. Plans, Elevations, and Sections, of the *Houfe of Correction* for the County of *Middlefex*, to be erected in Co'd Bath Fields, London; together with the Particular of the feveral Materials to be contracted for, and manner of ufing the fame in building.

N. B. This Work is engraved from the original defigns, and publifhed with the authority of the magiftrates, by *Charles Middleton*, Architect, engraved on 53 plates, imperial folio, price 2l. 12s. 6d. half bound.

4. *The Cabinet Maker and Upholfterer's Guide*; or Repofitory of Defigns for every article of houfehold furniture, in the neweft and moft approved tafte: difplaying a great variety of patterns for Chairs, Stools, Sofas, Confidante, Duchelfe, Side Boards, Pedeftals and Vafes, Cellerets, Knife Cafes, Defk and Book Cafes, Secretary and Book Cafes, Library Cafes, Library Tables, Reading Defks, Chefts of Drawers,

[2]

Urn Stands, Tea Caddies, Tea Trays, Card Tables, Pier Tables, Pembroke Tables, Tambour Tables, Dressing Glasses, Dressing Table- and Drawers, Commodes, Rudd's Table, Bidets, Night Tables, Bason Stands, Wardrobes, Pot Cupboards, Brackets, Hanging Shelves, Fire Screens, Beds, Field Beds, Sweep Tops for ditto, Bed Pillars, Candle Stands, Lamps, Pier Glasses, Terms for Busts, Cornices for Library Cases, Wardrobes, &c. at large, ornamented Tops for Pier Tables, Pembroke Tables, Commodes, &c. &c. in the plainest and most enriched styles, with a scale to each, and an explanation in letter-press. Also the Plan of a Room, shewing the proper distribution of the furniture. The whole exhibiting near three hundred different designs, engraved on one hundred and twenty-six folio plates: from drawings by *A. Heppelwhite & Co.* Cabinet-Makers, 2l. 2s. bound.

5. *The Builder's Price Book;* containing a correct list of the prices allowed by the most eminent surveyors in London to the several artificers concerned in building; including *the journeymen's prices.* A new edition, corrected, with great additions, by an experienced surveyor, 2s. 6d. sewed.

6. *Familiar Architecture:* consisting of original Designs of Houses for Gentlemen and Tradesmen, Parsonages and Summer Retreats; with Back-Fronts, Sections, &c. together with Banqueting-Rooms, and Churches. To which is added, the Masonry of the Semicircular and Elliptical Arches, with practical Remarks. By the late *Thomas Rawlins,* Architect. On fifty-one Plates Royal Quarto. Price 1l. 1s.

7. *Crunden's Convenient and Ornamental Architecture*; consisting of original designs for plans, elevations, and sections, beginning with the farm-house, and regularly ascending to the most grand and magnificent villa; calculated both for town and country, and to suit all persons in every station of life; with a reference, and explanation in letter-press, of the use of every room in each separate building, and the dimensions accurately figured on the plans, with exact scales for the measurement; elegantly engraved on seventy copper-plates, 16s. bound.

8. *The Country Gentleman's Architect,* in a great variety of new designs for cottages farm-houses, country-houses, villas, lodges for park or garden entrances, and ornamental wooden gates; with plans of the offices belonging to each design; distributed with a strict attention to convenience, elegance, and economy. Engraved on thirty-two quarto plates, from designs drawn by *J. Miller,* Architect, 10s. 6d. sewed.

9. *Garret's Designs and Estimates for Farm-houses,* for the counties of York, Northumberland, Cumberland, Westmoreland, and the Bishoprick of Durham. Folio, 5s. sewed.

10. Dr.

[3]

10. *Dr. Brook Taylor's Method of Perspective made easy*, both in Theory and Practice; in two Books; being an attempt to make the Art of Perspective easy and familiar, to adapt it entirely to the Arts of Design, and to make an entertaining Study to any Gentleman who shall choose so polite an Amusement. By *Joshua Kirby*, Designer in Perspective to his Majesty, and Fellow of the Royal and Antiquarian Societies. Illustrated with thirty-five Copper Plates, correctly engraved under the Author's Inspection. The third Edition, with several Additions and Improvements. Elegantly printed on Imperial Paper, 1l. 10s. half bound.

11. The same work in two Volumes quarto, 1l. 1s.

12. *The Perspective of Architecture*, a work entirely new: deduced from the principles of Dr. Brook Taylor, and performed by two rules of universal application: illustrated with seventy-three plates. Begun by command of his present majesty when Prince of Wales. By *Joshua Kirby*, Designer in Perspective to his Majesty, and Fellow of the Royal and Antiquarian Societies. Elegantly printed on imperial paper, 1l. 16s. half bound.

13. *The Description and Use of a new Instrument called the Architectonic Sector*, by which any part of architecture may be drawn with facility and exactness. By *Joshua Kirby*, Designer in Perspective to his Majesty, and Fellow of the Royal and Antiquarian Societies. Illustrated with twenty-five plates. Elegantly printed on imperial paper, 1l. 1s. half bound.

14. The two Frontispieces, by Hogarth, to Kirby's Perspective, may be had separate, at 5s. each.

15. *The Carpenter's and Joiner's Repository*; or, a new System of Lines and Proportions for Doors, Windows, Chimnies, Cornices and Mouldings, for finishing of rooms, &c. &c. A great variety of stair-cases, on a plan entirely new, and easy to be understood. Circular Circular Soffits, skewing and winding in straight and circular Walls, Groins, Angle Brackets, circular and elliptical Sky-Lights, and the method of squaring and preparing their circular Bars, Shop Fronts, &c. By *W. Pain*, Joiner. Engraved on sixty-nine folio copper-plates, 16s. bound.

16. *Pain's British Palladio, or the Builder's General Assistant*; demonstrating, in the most easy and practical method, all the principal rules of architecture, from the ground plan to the ornamental finish. Illustrated with several new and useful designs of houses, with their plans, elevations, and sections. Also clear and ample instructions annexed to each subject, in letter-press; with a list of prices for materials and labour,

[4]

and labour only. *This work will be universally useful to all carpenters, bricklayers, masons, joiners, plaisterers, and others, concerned in the several branches of building, &c.* comprehending the following subjects, viz. Plans, elevations and sections of gentlemen's houses. Designs for doors, chimneys, and ceilings, with their proper embellishments, in the most modern taste. A great variety of mouldings, for base and surbase architraves, imposts, friezes, and cornices, with their proper ornaments for practice, drawn to half size: to which are added, scales for enlarging or lessening at pleasure, if required. Also, great variety of stair-cases; shewing the practical method of executing them, in any case required, viz. groins, angle-brackets, circular circular flewing and winding soffits, domes, sky-lights, &c. all made plain and easy to the meanest capacity. The proportion of windows for the light to rooms. Preparing foundations; the proportion of chimneys to rooms, and sections of flews. The principal timbers properly laid out on each plan, viz. the manner of framing the roofs, and finding the length and backing of hips, either square or bevel. Scantlings of the timbers, figured in proportion to their bearing. The method of trussing girders, scarfing plates, &c. and many other articles, particularly useful to all persons in the building profession. The whole correctly engraved on forty-two folio copper-plates, from the original designs of *William* and *James Pain.* Price 16s. bound.

N. B. This is PAIN's last work.

17. *The Practical Builder*, or Workman's General Assistant; shewing the most approved and easy methods for drawing and working the whole or separate part of any building; as, the Use of the Tramel for Groins, Angle Brackets, Niches, &c. semi-circular arches on flewing Jambs, the preparing and making their soffits; rules of carpentry, to find the length and backing of straight or curved hips, trusses for roofs, domes, &c. Trussing of girders, section of floors, &c. The proportion of the five orders in their general and particular parts: gluing of columns; stair-cases, with their ramp and twisted rails, fixing their carriages, newels, &c. Frontispieces, chimney-pieces, ceilings, cornices, architraves, &c. in the newest taste; with plans and elevations of gentlemen's and farm-houses, barns, &c. By *W. Pain*, Architect and Joiner. Engraved on eighty-three quarto plates, 12s. bound. A new edition, with improvements by the author.

18. *The Carpenter's Pocket Directory*; containing the best methods of framing timbers of all figures and dimensions, with their several parts; as floors, roofs in ledgments, their length and backings; trussed roofs, spires and domes; trussing

girders,

girders, partitions, and bridges, with abutments; centering for arches, vaults, &c. cutting stone ceilings, groins, &c. with their moulds: centres for drawing Gothic arches, ellipses, &c. With the plan and sections of a barn. Engraved on twenty-four plates, with explanations, forming the most complete and useful work of the kind yet published. By *W. Pain*, Architect and Carpenter, 4s. bound.

19. *Designs in Architecture*; consisting of plans, elevations, and sections, for temples, baths, casines, pavilions, garden seats, obelisks, and other buildings: for decorating pleasure-grounds, parks, forests, &c. &c. By *John Soan*. Engraved on thirty-eight copper-plates, imperial octavo, 6s. sewed.

20. *Grotesque Architecture*, or Rural Amusement; consisting of plans, elevations and sections, for huts, summer and winter hermitages, retreats, terminaries, Chinese, Gothic, and natural grottoes, cascades, rustic seats, barns, mosques, moresque pavilions, grotesque seats, green houses, &c. many of which may be executed with flints, irregular stones, rude branches and roots of trees; containing twenty-eight new designs, with scales to each. By *W. Wright*, Architect. Octavo, 4s. 6d. sewed.

21. *The Temple Builder's most useful Companion*: containing original designs in the Greek, Roman, and Gothic taste. By *C. T. Overton*. Engraved on fifty copper-plates, octavo, 7s. sewed.

22. *The Carpenter's Treasure*; a collection of designs for temples, with their plans; gates, doors, rails, and bridges, in the Gothic taste, with centres at large for striking Gothic curves and mouldings, and some specimens of rails in the Chinese taste, forming a complete system for rural decorations. By *N. Wallis*, Architect. Engraved on sixteen plates, octavo, 2s. 6d. sewed.

23. *The Modern Joiner*; or, a Collection of Original Designs, in the present taste, for chimney-pieces and door-cases, with their mouldings and enrichments at large; friezes, tablets, ornaments for pilasters, bases, sub-bases and cornices for rooms, &c. with a table, shewing the proportion of chimnies, with their entablatures, to rooms of any size. By *N. Wallis*, Architect. Quarto, 8s.

24. *Ornaments in the Palmyrene Taste*; engraved on twelve quarto plates. By *N. Wallis*, 4s. 6d. sewed.

25. *Currus Civilis*, or Genteel Designs for coaches, chariots, post-chaises, vis-à-vis, road and park phaetons, whiskies, single horse chaises, &c. Elegantly engraved on thirty plates. Quarto, 10s. 6d. sewed.

26. *A New Book of Ornaments*; containing a variety of elegant

[6]

elegant defigns for modern pannels, commonly executed in ftucco, wood, or painting, and ufed in decorating principal rooms. Drawn and etched by *P. Columbani*. Quarto, 7s. 6d. fewed.

27. *A Variety of Capitals, Frizes and Cornices*; how to increafe or decreafe them, ftill retaining the fame proportion as the original. Likewife, twelve defigns for chimney-pieces, drawn an inch and a half to a foot. On twelve plates, drawn and etched by *P. Columbani*. Folio, 6s. fewed.

28. *An Effay on the Conftruction and Building of Chimnies*, including an enquiry into the common caufes of their fmoaking, and the moft effectual remedies for removing fo intolerable a nuifance; with a table to proportion chimnies to the fize of the room. Illuftrated with proper figures. A new edition. By *Robert Clavering*, Builder, 2s. 6d. fewed.

29. *The Manner of Securing all Sorts of Buildings from Fire*; a treatife upon the conftruction of arches made with bricks and plaifter, called flat arches, and of a roof without timber, called a brick roof; with fome letters that paffed between the Count D'Efpie, Peter Wyche, and William Beckford, Efqrs. on this fubject. Octavo, 2s. fewed.

30. *Langley's Builder's Director*, or Bench Mate; being a pocket treafury of the Grecian, Roman and Gothic orders of architecture, made eafy to the meaneft capacity, by near 500 examples, engraved on 184 copper-plates. 12mo. 4s. bound.

31. *Every Man a Complete Builder*; or eafy Rules and Proportions for drawing and working the feveral parts of architecture. In which are given a plan, elevation, and fection of the curious truffed carpenter's work, erected to fupport the centre arch of Black-Friars Bridge, from an exact meafurement. Compiled by *Edward Oakley*. Octavo, 4s. 6d. fewed.

32. *The Joiner and Cabinet Maker's Darling*; containing fixty different defigns for all forts of frets, frizes, &c. 3s. fewed.

33. *The Carpenter's Companion*; containing thirty-three defigns for all forts of Chinefe railing and gates. Octavo, 2s. fewed.

34. *The Carpenter's Complete Guide* to the whole Syftem of Gothic Railing; containing thirty-two new defigns, with fcales to each. Octavo, 2s. fewed.

35. *The Carpenter and Joiner's Vade Mecum*, by *Robert Clavering* and Company, 2s. fewed.

36. *A Geometrical View of the Five Orders of Columns in Architecture*, adjufted by aliquot parts; whereby the meaneft capacity,

[7]

capacity, by infpection, may delineate and work an entire order, or any part, of any magnitude required. On a large fheet, 1s.

37. *Elevation of the New Bridge at Black-Friars*, with plan of the foundation and fuperftructure, by R. *Baldwin*, 12 inches by 48 inches, 5s.

38. *Plans, Elevations, and Sections* of the Machines and Centering, ufed in erecting Black-Friars Bridge; drawn and engraved by R. *Baldwin*, clerk of the work; on feven large plates, with explanations in French and Englifh. Price 10s. 6d. or, with the elevation, 15s.

39. Elevation of the *Stone Bridge* built over the Severn, at *Skrewſbury*; with plan of the foundation and fuperftructure, elegantly engraved by Rooker. Price 1s. 6d.

40. Plans, Elevations, and Section of the *Gaol, Bridewell, and Sheriff's Ward*, lately built at *Bodmin*, in the county of Cornwall, by *John Call*, Efq. upon the plan recommended by *John Howard*, Efq. On a large fheet. Price 2s. 6d.

41. *London and Weſtminſter improved.* Illuſtrated by plans. To which is prefixed, a difcourfe on public magnificence; with obfervations on the ftate of arts and artifts in this kingdom, wherein the ftudy of the polite arts is recommended as neceffary to a liberal education: concluded by fome propofals relative to places not laid down in the plans. By *John Gwynn*, Architect. Price 5s. in boards.

42. Plans, Elevations, and Sections, prefented to the *corporation of Bath*, for the improvement of the *baths* in that city; intending to make the whole one grand, uniform, elegant and convenient ftructure of the Ionic order. By the late R. *Dingley*, Efq. Engraved on nine folio plates, by Rooker, &c. Price 6s. fewed.

43. *Encauſtic*, or Count Caylus's Method of painting in the manner of the Ancients. By J. H. Mantz. Octavo, 5s. bound.

44. *The Young Draftſman's Guide* to the true Outlines of the Human Figure; or a great variety of eafy examples of the Human Body; calculated to encourage young beginners, and thereby lead to the habit of drawing with accuracy and facility, on true principles. By an *eminent artiſt*, deceafed. Engraved on eighteen copper-plates. Folio. Price 5s. fewed.

The following books, in the prefent tafte of ornament, are ufeful to all carvers, ſtucco-workers, &c.

45. *The Principles of Drawing Ornaments* made eafy, by proper examples of leaves for mouldings, capitals, fcrolls, hufks, foliage, &c. engraved in imitation of drawings, on fixteen plates. With inftructions for learning without a mafter. Particularly ufeful to carvers, cabinet-makers, ftucco-workers,

painters,

[8]

painters, smiths, and every one concerned in ornamental decorations. By an artist. Quarto, 4s. 6d. sewed.

46. *Ornamental Iron Work*; or designs in the present taste, for fan lights, stair-case railing, window guard irons, lamp irons, palisades and gates. With a scheme for adjusting designs with facility and accuracy to any slope. Engraved on 21 plates. Quarto, 6s. sewed.

47. *A new Book of Ornaments*: by S. Alken. On six plates. 2s. 6d. sewed.

48. Twelve new designs of frames for Looking-Glasses, Pictures, &c. by S. H. carver, 2s. sewed.

49. *A Book of Tablets*, done to the full size commonly used for chimney-pieces. Designed and etched by *J. Pether*, on six plates, 3s. 6d. sewed.

50. Law's new book of Ornaments, 2s. sewed.

51. A book of Vases, by *T. Law*, 2s. sewed.

52. A book of Vases, by P. *Columbani*, 2s. sewed.

53. A book of Vases from the antique, on twelve plates, 2s. sewed.

54. *Gerard's* new book of Foliage, 2s. sewed.

55. A small book of Ornaments, on six leaves, by *G. Edwards*, 1s. sewed.

56. A new book of Designs for Girandoles and Glass Frames. Drawn and engraved by *B. Pastorini*, on ten plates, 4s. sewed.

57. An Interior View of *Durham Cathedral*, and a View of the elegant *Gothic Shrine* in said Cathedral. Elegantly engraved on two large Sheets, size 19 and a half by 22 and a half. Price 12s. the pair.

58. A Plan and Elevation of the King of Portugal's palace at Mafra, on two large sheets, 6s.

59. A north-west View of Greenwich Church, 1s.

60. An elegant engraved View of Shoreditch Church, 2 feet 4 inches by 1 foot 8 inches, 3s.

61. The Art of Practical Measuring by the Sliding Rule; shewing how to measure timber, stone, board, glass, painting, &c. also gauging, &c. by H. Coggeshall. A new edition, by J. Ham, 1s. bound.

62. *The Building Act of the 14th Geo. III.* With plates, shewing the proper thickness of party walls, external walls, and chimneys. A complete index, list of surveyors and their residence, &c. in a small pocket size, 2s. 6d. sewed.

N. B. The notice and certificate required by the above act, may be had printed with blank spaces for filling up, price 2d. each, or 13 for 2s.

www.ingramcontent.com/pod-product-compliance
Lightning Source LLC
Chambersburg PA
CBHW020129170426
43199CB00010B/700